THE RISK OF BLACK SWANS

What Larry writes is always worth reading, and Reducing the Risk of Black Swans is no exception. Both a valuable wake-up call regarding the reality of today's markets and an insightful guide to the "'science of investing," results in his delivering on his promise to help the reader "learn how you can minimize the risks of incurring large losses in your investment portfolio while still allowing you to keep the portfolio's expected returns at the level that could be expected from a market-like portfolio." Buy it, read it and you and/or your clients will be well rewarded.

— **HAROLD EVENSKY, PRESIDENT, EVENSKY & KATZ**

A useful, quick and convincing read. A treasured complement to my collection of Swedroe books.

— **ED TOWER, PROFESSOR OF ECONOMICS, DUKE UNIVERSITY**

REDUCING THE RISK OF
BLACK
SWANS

REDUCING THE RISK OF
BLACK SWANS

USING THE SCIENCE OF INVESTING TO
CAPTURE RETURNS WITH LESS VOLATILITY

LARRY SWEDROE & KEVIN GROGAN

BAM ALLIANCE Press
8182 Maryland Ave
Suite 500
St. Louis, MO 63105
thebamalliance.com

Design by Alan Dubinsky

CONTENTS

ACKNOWLEDGMENTS

Books are rarely the work of just one (or in this case, two) author(s). We would like to thank our colleagues at Buckingham, Adam Birenbaum, Jared Kizer, David Levin, Laura Latragna and Vladimir Maşek for all their support and encouragement.

Larry adds: I would also like to thank my wife Mona, the love of my life. Walking through life with her has truly been a gracious experience.

Kevin adds: My family, Julie and Ryan, make every day a joy. I thank my parents Bob and Nancy, and my brother Mark and sister-in-law Ashley, who have always supported me and had my best interests in mind.

INTRODUCTION

This book was written for those looking to expand their knowledge of the evidence-based investing world. In this world, peer-reviewed research and academia are used to design portfolios, not instincts, opinions or ego. Whether you are an advisor looking to better serve your clients, an investor looking to become more knowledgeable on the workings of your portfolio, or even a financial oracle, you will benefit from this book. While it is short in length, its content is heavy. It is data-rich and full of detailed examples. The empty rhetoric or the distracting noise often heard in the active investment world has no place here. Science and hard data make our case. There is no need for elaborate prose or the hyperbolic statements so often heard on the other side of the investing aisle.

You are about to embark on a journey that we hope will be both informative and of great value. It is a roadmap to the Holy Grail of investing — the search for an investment strategy that can deliver higher returns without increased risk or the same return with reduced risk.

Finally, if you tend to be daunted by data or unfamiliar terms, don't worry. We have made great efforts to explain concepts in as simple terms as possible. Take your time, and know that by reading this book, you are taking steps toward becoming a better, more informed, hands-on investor. And that is something of which you can be proud.

CHAPTER 1:
HOW TO THINK ABOUT
EXPECTED STOCK RETURNS

An important part of the process of developing an investment plan is estimating future returns to stocks and bonds. Unfortunately, many investors make two big mistakes when doing so. The first mistake is to simply extrapolate past returns into the future. The reason that is a mistake is because it ignores the fact that current stock valuations play a very important role in determining future returns. Consider the following.

From 1926 through 1979, the S&P 500 Index returned 9.0 percent. From 1980 through 1999 it returned 17.9 percent, raising the return over the full period by 2.3 percent to 11.3 percent. Investors using the historical return of 11.3 percent as a predictor of future returns where highly likely to be disappointed because they failed to take into account the fact that the earnings yield (the inverse of the price/earnings ratio) had fallen all the way from 11.4 percent to 3.5 percent! And lower earnings yields predict lower, not higher, future returns.

While the historical *real* return to stocks has been 6.8 percent (9.8 percent nominal return minus 3.0 percent inflation) most financial economists are now forecasting real returns well below that. While there is no generally agreed upon best metric for estimating future returns, the Shiller CAPE 10 (cyclically adjusted price-to-earnings ratio) is considered by many to be at least as good, if not better, than other metrics as it explains a significant portion of the variation in future returns. The CAPE 10 ratio uses smoothed real earnings to eliminate the fluctuations in net income caused by variations in profit margins over a typical business cycle.

The first to argue for smoothing a firm's earnings over a longer term were value investors Benjamin Graham and David Dodd. In their classic text, *Security Analysis*, Graham and Dodd noted one-year earnings were too volatile to offer a good idea of a firm's true earning power. Decades later, Yale economist and Nobel Prize winner Robert Shiller popularized the 10-year version of Graham and Dodd's P/E as a way to value the stock market.

In an attempt to minimize the impact of what might be *temporarily* very low earnings (due to a recession) or very high earnings (due to a boom), the Shiller CAPE 10 smoothes out earnings by taking the average of the last 10 years' earnings, and adjusts that figure for inflation. Let us assume that the Shiller CAPE 10 is at 23.9 (which it was as we wrote this), well above its historical average. To estimate future returns using this metric you take the earnings yield — the inverse of the Shiller CAPE ratio — and you get 4.2 percent. However, because the Shiller PE is based on the lagged 10-year earnings, we need to make an adjustment for the historical growth in real earnings, which is about 1.5 percent per year. To make that adjustment we then multiply the 4.2 percent earnings yield by 1.075 (0.015 x 5), producing an estimated real return to stocks of about 4.5 percent, or 2.3 percent below the historical return. (We multiply by five because a 10-year average figure lags current earnings by five years.) Other methodologies (such as using what is called the Gordon Constant Growth Dividend Discount Model) come up with similar results, with most financial economists forecasting real future returns in the range of about 4 to 5 percent.

3

The second mistake investors make is treating the expected return as "deterministic" — they will earn that specific return — rather than as just the mean of a potentially very wide dispersion of potential returns. The following demonstrates why thinking of the expected return in a deterministic way is dangerous.

In a November 2012 paper, "An Old Friend: The Stock Market's Shiller PE," Cliff Asness of AQR Capital found that the Shiller CAPE 10 does provide us with valuable information. Specifically, he found that 10-year forward average real returns fall nearly monotonically as starting Shiller P/Es increase. He also found that as the starting Shiller CAPE 10 increased, worst cases became worse and best cases became weaker. And he found that while the metric provided valuable insights there were still very wide dispersions of returns. For example:

- When the CAPE 10 was below 9.6, 10-year forward real returns averaged 10.3 percent. In relative terms, that is more than 50 percent above the historical average of 6.8 percent (9.8 percent nominal return less 3.0 percent inflation). The best 10-year real return was 17.5 percent. The worst was still a pretty good 4.8 percent real return, just 2.0 percent below the average, and 29 percent below it in relative terms. The range between the best and worst outcomes was a 12.7 percent difference in real returns.

- When the CAPE 10 was between 15.7 and 17.3 (about its average of 16.5), the 10-year forward real return averaged 5.6 percent. The best and worst 10-year forward returns were 15.1 percent and 2.3 percent, respectively. The range between the best and worst outcomes was a 12.8 percent difference in real returns.

- When the CAPE 10 was between 21.1 and 25.1, the 10-year forward real return averaged just 0.9 percent. The best 10-year forward real return was still 8.3 percent, above the historical average of 6.8. However, the worst 10-year forward real return was now −4.4 percent. The range between the best and worst outcomes was a difference of 12.7 percent in real terms.

- When the CAPE 10 was above 25.1, the real return over the following 10 years averaged just 0.5 percent — virtually the same as the long-term real return on the risk-free benchmark, one-month Treasury bills. The best 10-year real return was 6.3 percent, just 0.5 percent below the historical average. But, the worst 10-year real return was now −6.1 percent. The range between the best and worst outcomes was a difference of 12.4 percent in real terms.

What can we learn from the above data? First, starting valuations clearly matter, and they matter a lot. Higher starting values mean that future expected returns are lower, and vice versa. However, there is still a wide dispersion of potential outcomes for which we must prepare when developing an investment plan.

The illustration below shows the right way to think about the expected return of a portfolio, an asset class or an individual stock. Although returns are not actually normally distributed (they are log normally distributed), we think this illustration will be helpful in explaining how to think about expected returns.

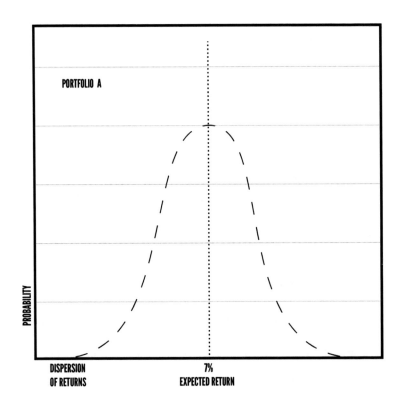

In the illustration, think of Portfolio A as a market-like portfolio (such as the Vanguard Total Stock Market Fund). Using the 4.5 percent expected real return to stocks (based on the Shiller CAPE 10) and an expected inflation rate of 2.5 percent we arrive at an expected return of 7 percent for the overall stock market. The right way to think about the 7 percent figure is that it is just the *mean (and median)* of the wide dispersion depicted. In other words, there is a 50 percent chance the return will be above the expected 7 percent, perhaps a 30 percent chance it will be above 9 percent, a 10 percent chance it will be above 12 percent and a 5 percent chance it will be above 13 percent. And there are similar possibilities that it will fall on the left side of the distribution with returns below, and even well below, the expected rate of 7 percent.

Now consider Portfolio B, which has the same 7 percent expected return, but a different potential dispersion of returns. As the illustration on the following page shows, more of the weight of the distribution (the probability density) is closer to the mean return of 7 percent than is the case with Portfolio A — it is a taller and thinner bell curve, with less of the weight in the tails, both left (bad) and right (good).

7

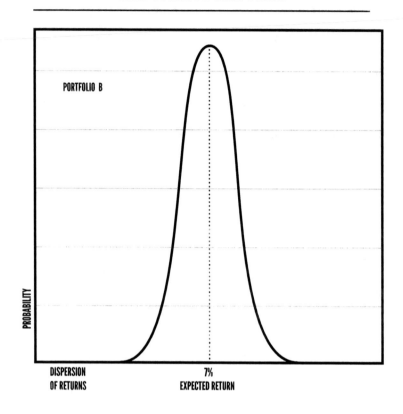

Now consider both Portfolios A and B. They have the same expected return — in both cases the mean return is 7 percent. However, they have a different dispersion of returns. If you were faced with the choice of living with the risks of the potential dispersions of returns of either Portfolio A or B, which would you choose?

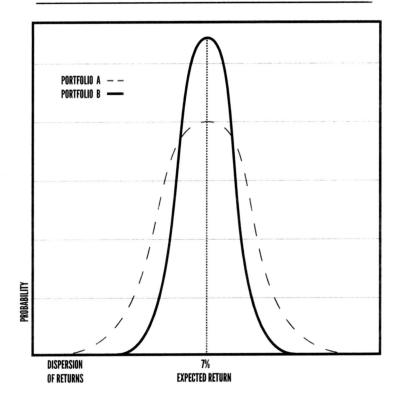

If you are like most people you would choose to live with the risks of Portfolio B. The reason is that most people are risk averse — given the same expected return, they choose the portfolio with the lower standard deviation of returns (Portfolio B). Said another way, if you are like most people you are willing to sacrifice the opportunity to earn the great returns in the right tail of the distribution of Portfolio A (that are not there with Portfolio B) if you also minimize, or eliminate, the risk of the very bad returns in the left tail of Portfolio A (that are not there with Portfolio B).

Are you interested in learning how to create portfolios where the distribution of potential returns looks more like Portfolio B than Portfolio A? Learning how we have been doing this for about 20 years for our clients is the journey we will take you on, beginning with a history of modern financial theory and asset pricing models.

CHAPTER 2:
A BRIEF HISTORY OF
MODERN FINANCIAL THEORY

The birth of modern finance can be traced back to 1952, when Harry

Markowitz's paper "Portfolio Selection" was published in *The Journal*

of Finance. The most important aspect of this work was that Markowitz

showed that it is not a security's own risk and expected return that is

important to an investor, but rather the contribution the security makes

to the risk and expected return of the investor's entire portfolio. This

contribution depends not only on the riskiness of the security itself, but

also on how the security behaves relative to how the other assets in

the portfolio behave (the correlation of their returns). Markowitz was

able to show that you could add risky, and higher expected returning, assets to a portfolio without increasing the portfolio's overall risk if the asset's returns were not perfectly correlated with the other assets in the portfolio.

William Sharpe and John Lintner are typically given most of the credit for introducing the Capital Asset Pricing Model (CAPM). The CAPM was the first formal asset pricing model, and it was built on ideas from Markowitz's paper. The CAPM provided the first precise definition of risk and how it drives expected returns.

The CAPM looks at returns through a "one-factor" lens, meaning that the risk and return of a portfolio is determined only by its exposure to beta. It's important to understand that beta is not the stock allocation of a portfolio. It is the measure of the equity-type risk of a stock, mutual fund or portfolio, relative to the risk of the overall market. An asset (or portfolio) with a beta above 1 has more equity-type risk than the overall market. If it has a beta below 1 it has less equity-type risk than the overall market. Thus, a portfolio with a 70 percent allocation to stocks and 30 percent allocation to Treasury bills could have a beta of 1 if the stocks in the portfolio were highly risky stocks with a beta of about 1.4. For example, these stocks might be high flying tech stocks. Conversely, a portfolio with a 100 percent allocation to stocks could have a beta of just 0.7 if the stocks it held were all less risky than the market as a whole. Perhaps they are "defensive" stocks such as utilities, drug store chains and supermarket chains.

The CAPM was the finance world's operating model for about 30 years. However, all models by definition are flawed, or wrong. If they were perfectly correct they would be laws, like we have in physics. Over time, anomalies that violated the CAPM began to surface. Among the more prominent ones were:

- 1981: Rolf Banz's "The Relationship Between Return and Market Value of Common Stocks" was published in *The Journal of Financial Economics*. Banz found that beta does not fully explain the higher average return of small (or lower market capitalization) stocks.

- 1981: Sanjoy Basu's "The Relationship Between Earnings' Yield, Market Value and Return for NYSE Common Stocks," published in *The Journal of Financial Economics*, found that the positive relationship between the earnings yield (earnings/price) and average return is left unexplained by beta.

- 1985: Barr Rosenburg, Kenneth Reid and Ronald Lanstein found a positive relationship between average stock return and book-to-market ratio in their 1985 paper "Persuasive Evidence of Market Inefficiency" published in *The Journal of Portfolio Management*.

- 1988: Laxmi Chand Bhandari's "Debt/Equity Ratio and Expected Common Stock Returns: Empirical Evidence" published in *The Journal of Finance* found that firms with high leverage have higher average returns than firms with low leverage.

Eugene Fama and Kenneth French's 1992 paper "The Cross-Section of Expected Stock Returns" summarized all of these anomalies in one place. The essential conclusions from the paper were that the CAPM only explained about two-thirds of the differences in returns of diversified portfolios, and that a better model could be built using more than just the one factor of beta.

THE FAMA-FRENCH THREE-FACTOR MODEL

One year later, Fama and French published "Common Risk Factors in the Returns on Stocks and Bonds" in *The Journal of Financial Economics*. This paper proposed a new asset pricing model, called the Fama-French Three-Factor model. This model proposes that along with the market factor of beta, exposure to the factors of size and value explain the cross-section of expected stock returns. The essential takeaway from this research is that small-cap and value stocks are riskier than large-cap and growth stocks, and that risk is compensated for with higher expected returns.

14

The authors demonstrated that we live not in a one-factor world, but in a three-factor world. They showed that the risk and expected return of a portfolio is explained by not only its exposure to beta, but also by its exposure to two other factors: size (small-cap stocks) and price (stocks with low relative prices, or value stocks). Fama and French hypothesized that while small-cap and value stocks have higher betas — more equity-type risk — they also have additional unique risks that are unrelated to beta. Thus, small-cap and value stocks are riskier than large-cap and growth stocks, explaining their higher historical returns and implying that such stocks should have higher expected returns in the future. Studies have confirmed that the three-factor model explains an overwhelming majority of the returns of diversified portfolios. In fact, the Fama-French model improved the explanatory power from about two-thirds of the differences in returns between diversified portfolios to more than 90 percent. An indirect, but important, implication of this finding was that if more than 90 percent of a diversified portfolio's returns could be explained by the portfolio's exposure to these factors, there wasn't much room left for active security selection or market timing to add value. The conclusion that could then be drawn was that passive investing was the strategy most likely to allow you to achieve your financial goals.

Subsequent research on the performance and persistence of performance of active managers supports that conclusion.

THE THREE FACTORS

Before looking at the returns to the three factors of beta, size and value, we need to go over a few key points. The first is that when looking at the returns to factors, they are always expressed in terms of *annual average* returns, not compound, or *annualized* returns — if we have 86 years of data, we take the sum of the returns in each of the 86 years and divide the total by 86. The second point is that they are always considered long-short portfolios. Thus:

- The beta factor is the *average annual* return on the total stock market (the long) *minus* the *average annual* return on Treasury bills (the short). From 1927 through 2013, the *average annual* return of market beta has been 8.3 percent.

- The small factor is the *annual average* return on small-cap stocks (the long) *minus* the *average annual* return on large-cap stocks (the short). Using the Center for Research in Securities Prices at the University of Chicago (CRSP) data, small-cap stocks are stocks in deciles 6–10 and large-cap stocks are those in deciles 1–5. From 1927 through 2013, small companies have outperformed large companies by an *annual average* of 3.6 percent per year.

- The value (or price) factor is the average annual return on value stocks (the long) minus the *average annual* return on growth stocks (the short). Ranking stocks by their book-to-market values, value stocks are the 30 percent of stocks with the highest book-to-market values and growth stocks are the 30 percent with the lowest book-to-market values. From 1927 through 2013, value companies have outperformed growth companies by an *annual average* of 4.9 percent per year.

INDEPENDENT RISK FACTORS

An important contribution by Fama and French was that they showed that size and price (value) are independent (unique) risk factors in that they provide investors with exposure to different risks than those provided by exposure to market risk (beta). Evidence of this independence can be seen when we examine the historical correlations of the size and price factors to the market factor. High correlations would mean the risk factors would be relatively good substitutes for each other. If that were the case, while investors could increase the expected return (and risk) of the portfolio by increasing their exposure to these risk factors, there would be little real diversification benefit. If the correlations are low, investors could both increase expected returns for a given level of risk and gain a diversification benefit. Thus, finding factors with low correlation provides us with valuable information we can use to build more efficient portfolios.

Since most people have an incorrect understanding of the term correlation (even most of the professional advisors we have met), before looking at the data we need to make sure that you know and understand the definitions of positive and negative correlation.

There is a positive correlation between two assets when one asset produces above-average returns (relative to its average) and the other asset *tends to* also produce above-average returns (relative to its average). The stronger the tendency, the closer the correlation will be to +1.

While most people seem to believe that negative correlation means that when one asset increases in value the other falls in value, it actually means that when one asset produces above-average returns (relative to its average), the other asset *tends to* produce below-average returns (relative to its average). The stronger the tendency, the closer the correlation will be to –1.

If the correlation is 0, two assets would be said to be uncorrelated. That means that when one asset produces above-average returns relative to its average, the other asset is just as likely to also produce above-average returns relative to its average as it is likely to produce below-average returns relative to its average.

The following examples will help clarify this concept.

EXAMPLE 1: Consider two assets A and B and their returns over a 10-year period. Their return series is depicted in the table below.

ASSET	YEAR 1	YEAR 2	YEAR 3	YEAR 4	YEAR 5	YEAR 6	YEAR 7	YEAR 8	YEAR 9	YEAR 10
A	12	8	12	8	12	8	12	8	12	8
B	8	12	8	12	8	12	8	12	8	12

Both assets A and B have an annual average return of 10. Whenever A's return is above its average of 10, B's return is below its average of 10. And whenever A's return is below its average of 10, B's return is above its average of 10. Thus, the assets are negatively correlated. Note that they are negatively correlated even though they both always produce positive returns.

EXAMPLE 2:

ASSET	YEAR 1	YEAR 2	YEAR 3	YEAR 4	YEAR 5	YEAR 6	YEAR 7	YEAR 8	YEAR 9	YEAR 10
A	2	–2	2	–2	2	–2	2	–2	2	–2
B	–2	2	–2	2	–2	2	–2	2	–2	2

Both assets in this series have an average annual return of 0 percent. Whenever A's return is above its average of 0, B's return is below its average of 0. Whenever A's return is below its average of 0, B's return is above its average of 0. Thus, again we see that the two assets are negatively correlated.

Now comes the fun part. We will now string together the two examples so that we have a 20-year period. The first 10 years are the returns from Example 1, and the second 10 years are from Example 2. Thus, the return series looks like this:

ASSET A: 12, 8, 12, 8, 12, 8, 12, 8, 12, 8, 2, –2, 2, –2, 2, –2, 2, –2, 2, –2.

ASSET B: 8, 12, 8, 12, 8, 12, 8, 12, 8, 12, –2, 2, –2, 2, –2, 2, –2, 2, –2, 2.

Recall that both A and B had average returns in the first 10 years of 10 percent, and average returns of 0 percent in the second 10 years. Thus, their average return for the full 20 years in both cases is 5 percent. Now recall our definitions. If you are not sure, go back and read them again before attempting to answer the question: Are A and B positively or negatively correlated?

With the definitions in mind, we see that whenever A's return was above its average of 5, B's return was also above its average of 5. And whenever A's return was below its average of 5, B's return was also below its average of 5. Thus, we see that despite the fact that A and B were negatively correlated over each of the two 10-year periods, over the full 20-year period they were positively correlated. Besides illustrating the concepts of positive and negative correlation, we hope you also come away with the understanding that you need long-term data series for correlations to have any real meaning. In addition, it is important to understand that correlations of risky assets have a tendency to drift over time. And as 2008 demonstrated, the correlation of all risky assets has a nasty tendency to move toward 1 during crises. Thus, when considering an asset for inclusion in a portfolio you need to not only consider the asset's long-term correlation with other portfolio assets, but also consider when the correlation tends to rise and when it tends to fall.

With these important understandings, we now turn to examining the long-term correlation of the three factors. The data below shows the annual correlations of the returns of the three factors, market beta, size and value from 1927 through 2013.

MARKET BETA VS. SIZE: 0.42
MARKET BETA VS. VALUE: 0.10
SIZE VS. VALUE: 0.10

What we find is that the size factor has a correlation of about 0.4 to beta, or the market factor. Recalling our definitions, that means that there is a tendency, though not a very strong one, that whenever the market factor (the return of stocks minus the return of one-month Treasury bills) produces a return of above 8 percent (its average), small-cap stocks will outperform large-cap stocks by more than the average of 3.6 percent a year. That means that there will also be a significant number of years when the return on beta is above its average of 8.0 percent and the size premium will be below 3.6 percent, including many years when the size premium will be negative (large-cap stocks will outperform small-cap stocks).

We also see that the value factor has a correlation to the market factor of just 0.1. Recalling our definitions, that means that whenever the market factor is above 8.0 percent, there is only a very small tendency for the value premium to be more than its average of 4.9 percent.

We also see that the correlation of the size factor to the price factor was 0.1. Thus, there is a very small tendency (very close to a random event) that when the size premium is above 3.6 percent, the value premium will be above 4.9 percent.

We can see the low correlation of the factors by looking at the returns in the years 1998 and 2001. The table on the following page shows the returns of the S&P 500 Index and two asset class mutual funds from Dimensional Fund Advisors (DFA), the DFA Small Cap Portfolio and the

DFA Small Value Portfolio. The table also shows the return of a portfolio that has one-third of its assets in each of the three.

	S&P 500 INDEX	DFA SMALL CAP PORTFOLIO	DFA SMALL VALUE PORTFOLIO	EQUAL-WEIGHTED PORTFOLIO
1998	28.6	–5.5	–7.3	5.3
2001	–11.9	12.7	22.7	7.8

Note that the gap between the good and the bad years was 40.5 percent for the S&P 500 Index, 18.2 percent for the DFA Small Cap Portfolio and 30 percent for the DFA Small Value Portfolio, but just 2.5 percent for the equal-weighted portfolio. This simple example shows the benefits of diversifying across factors that have low correlation — you dampen the volatility of the portfolio. Dampening volatility is especially important to those in the withdrawal phase of their investment lifecycle when the order of returns matters a great deal because higher volatility can greatly increase the odds of outliving your assets.

The bottom line is that we find that our three factors have low correlations to each other. In fact, the size and value factors and the value and beta factors are virtually uncorrelated (their correlations are close to 0). That is good news. News we will use to build more efficient portfolios.

ACHIEVING YOUR GOALS IN A CAPM WORLD

In a CAPM (or one-factor) framework, the only ways to increase the expected return of your portfolio are to increase the allocation to stocks or to purchase higher beta stocks. In either case, you are not diversifying the sources of a portfolio's return — just adding more beta to the portfolio.

An example can illustrate this point. Let's assume equities (as represented by a total stock market fund) are expected to return 7 percent and bonds (as represented by the yield on say a five-year Treasury bond) are expected to return 5 percent. These figures are used to keep the math simple. Based upon your ability and willingness to take risk, you decide that a portfolio with an allocation of 50 percent stocks and 50 percent bonds would be appropriate. Such a portfolio would have an expected return of 6 percent. However, your financial plan in terms of desired spending requires a 6.5 percent return. In a one-factor world, in order to achieve the expected 6.5 percent return, basically you would have to increase your equity allocation to 75 percent.

PORTFOLIO 1: (75% X 7%) + (25% X 5%) = 6.5%

The only other alternative would be to increase the beta of the stocks in your portfolio. That would leave you owning a portfolio consisting of basically only very high beta stocks. In either case you would be adding more of the same beta risk that was already in your portfolio. Instead of having all your eggs in one risk basket (beta), would it not be better to diversify your sources of risk across other baskets with unique risks? Another important consideration is that the portfolio with 75 percent stocks is a lot more risky than the one with just 50 percent stocks — the allocation you felt was appropriate based on your risk tolerance.

ACHIEVING YOUR GOALS IN A THREE-FACTOR WORLD

Using the science of investing, there is an alternative way to increase the expected return of your portfolio. Since 1927, small value stocks have outperformed the market (as represented by the S&P 500 Index) by an *annualized* 3.8 percent. Thus, if we assume stocks will return 7 percent we might assume small value stocks will return an additional 3.8 percent a year, for a total return of 10.8 percent.

Recall our initial example of a 50 percent stock/50 percent bond allocation. Instead of increasing your stock allocation to achieve the higher 6.5 percent return, you decide to divide your 50 percent stock allocation equally between the S&P 500 Index and small value stocks — 25 percent each. Now the expected return is almost 7 percent.

PORTFOLIO 2: (25% X 7%) + (25% X 10.8%) + (50% X 5%) = 6.95%

Without increasing our stock allocation, we have increased the expected return to more than the required 6.5 percent. We did this by adding an allocation to the higher expected returning small value stocks. Thus, it is important to recognize that while our exposure to stocks basically remained unchanged (we did add an allocation of riskier small value stocks — though we did add two new unique risk factors, providing some diversification benefit), the expected return of the portfolio increased by more than did the risk. However, we don't need to earn 6.95 percent. Our plan only requires a return of 6.5 percent. With that in mind we can try lowering our stock allocation to perhaps 40 percent, again splitting the allocation equally between the S&P 500 Index and small value stocks. Now the expected return is:

PORTFOLIO 3: (20% X 7%) + (20% X 10.8%) + (60% X 5%) = 6.56%

We have now achieved our goal of an expected return of 6.5 percent. And we did so while only having an allocation to stocks of 40 percent. Using your intuition, which portfolio, Portfolio 1 or Portfolio 3, do you think is more risky? Which portfolio would you expect to perform worse in a bear market? Intuitively, most people will say Portfolio 1.

While Portfolio 3 has the same expected return as the 75 percent equity portfolio, the risks are completely different. Portfolios with higher equity allocations have greater potential for losses. The tradeoff is that the upside of the potential with higher equity allocations is much higher. For investors for whom the pain of a loss is greater than the benefit of an equal-sized gain, reducing downside risk at the price of reducing upside potential is a good trade-off.

There is another consideration especially important to loss-averse investors (which most are). Since bonds are safer investments than stocks, in a severe bear market the portfolio's maximum loss would likely be far lower with a 40 percent equity allocation than with a 75 percent one. 2008 provided a great example, at least if the bonds you owned were limited to Treasuries and other high-quality bonds. While the market fell 37 percent, five-year Treasury bonds rose about 13 percent. And Portfolio 3 not only owned less of the losing stocks, but it also owned far more of the winning bonds.

Using the S&P 500 Index, the Russell 2000 Value Index (for small-cap value stocks) and the five-year Treasury, we see that in 2008 Portfolio 1 would have lost 24.5 percent, Portfolio 2 9.9 percent and Portfolio 3 just 5.3 percent.

Thus, while the expected returns of the two portfolios are the same, the portfolio with the lower equity allocation has much less downside risk. Of course, the upside potential during a strong bull market is correspondingly lower. For example, in 2003 Portfolio 1 gained 35.1 percent, Portfolio 2 19.9 percent and Portfolio 3 just 16.4 percent.

For an investor for whom the pain of a loss is greater than the benefit of an equal-sized gain (probably you), reducing downside risk at the price of reducing upside potential is a good trade-off. To illustrate this point, examine the chart below.

DISTRIBUTION OF ANNUAL RETURNS 1979–2013

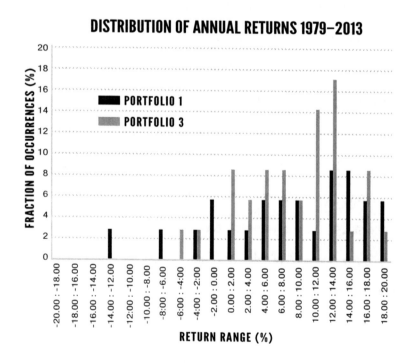

Portfolio 1 experienced more years where returns were on the left-hand side of the chart, as well as more years on the right-hand side of the chart — the tails were bigger.

CONSIDERATIONS

When constructing a portfolio — deciding on the right asset allocation — several factors should be given careful consideration. For example, you should consider how your labor capital correlates with the greater economic cycle risks of small-cap and value stocks compared to large-cap and growth stocks.

Another important consideration is a psychological one: the risk of tracking error regret. Tracking error is the amount by which the performance of a portfolio varies from that of the total market, or other broad market benchmark such as the S&P 500 Index. By diversifying across risk factors, investors take on increased tracking error risk because their portfolios look less like the market. While very few investors care when tracking error is positive (their portfolio beats the benchmark), many care when it is negative. Misery loves company. In other words, if your portfolio performs poorly because the market has performed poorly, at least you have company. On the other hand, if your portfolio is underperforming the market, you might begin to question your strategy, wondering why you are doing relatively poorly.

As you may recall, the year 1998 provided the perfect example of this as the DFA Small Value Portfolio underperformed the S&P 500 Index by about 36 percent. Such underperformance can test the mettle of even the most disciplined investors. Compounding the problem was that in order to adhere to your asset allocation plan you would have been required to rebalance the portfolio — selling some of the S&P 500 Index allocation (having just seen it gain almost 29 percent) to buy some of the poorly performing DFA Small Value Portfolio (which just lost more than 7 percent).

Because most investors are return chasers, they would be far more likely to increase their allocation to the S&P 500 Index and get rid of their small value allocation. Of course, doing so would be following a strategy of buying high and selling low — not exactly a prescription for investment success. It is why the evidence shows that investors, on average, underperform the very mutual funds in which they invest. On the other hand, those investors who remained disciplined and rebalanced would have been buying more small value stocks at low prices and selling some of their S&P 500 Index holdings high, a far more successful strategy. And it would have left them much better prepared for 2001 because they would have already sold some of their S&P 500 Index holdings (which then performed poorly) and increased their small value holdings (which performed well).

The bottom line is that to have a chance for positive tracking error, investors must accept the virtual certainty that negative tracking error will appear from time to time. Emotions associated with negative tracking error can lead investors to abandon carefully developed investment plans. Only those investors willing and able to accept tracking error risk should consider diversifying across the other risk factors.

In the next section, we will show you how you can utilize what you have learned to build more efficient portfolios. By combining the insights from Fama and French with Harry Markowitz's insight (for which he won a Nobel Prize) that you can add risky, but non-perfectly correlating assets to a portfolio and generate higher returns without a commensurate increase in the portfolio's volatility, we will show you how to build more efficient portfolios.

CHAPTER 3:
BUILDING A MORE
EFFICIENT PORTFOLIO

We will begin with a portfolio that has a conventional asset allocation of 60 percent S&P 500 Index and 40 percent five-year Treasury notes (the highest quality intermediate-term bond). The time frame will be the 39-year period 1975–2013. This period was chosen because it is the longest for which we have data on the indices we need. While maintaining the same 60 percent stock/40 percent bond allocation, we will then expand our investment universe to include other stock asset classes. We will see how the portfolio performed if one had the patience to stay with this allocation from 1975 through 2013 and rebalanced annually. We will then demonstrate how the portfolio's performance could have been made more efficient by increasing its diversification across asset classes. We do so in four simple steps. (Indices are not available for direct investment.)

PORTFOLIO 1

S&P 500 INDEX	**60%**
FIVE-YEAR TREASURY NOTES	**40%**

1975–2013

ANNUALIZED RETURN (%)	ANNUAL STANDARD DEVIATION (%)
10.8	10.6

By changing the composition of the control portfolio we will see how we can improve the efficiency of our portfolio. To avoid being accused of data mining, we will alter our allocations by arbitrarily "cutting things in half."

STEP 1: The first step is to diversify our stock holdings to include an allocation to U.S. small-cap stocks. Therefore, we reduce our allocation to the S&P 500 Index from 60 percent to 30 percent and allocate 30 percent to the Fama/French Small Cap Index. (The Fama-French indices use the academic definitions of asset classes. Note that regulated utilities and REITS have been excluded from the data.)

PORTFOLIO 2

S&P 500 INDEX	30%
FAMA/FRENCH SMALL CAP INDEX	30%
FIVE-YEAR TREASURY NOTES	40%

1975–2013

	ANNUALIZED RETURN (%)	ANNUAL STANDARD DEVIATION (%)
PORTFOLIO 1	10.8	10.6
PORTFOLIO 2	12.0	11.2

STEP 2: Our next step is to diversify our domestic stock holdings to include value stocks. We shift half of our 30 percent allocation in the S&P 500 Index to a large-cap value index and half of our 30 percent allocation of small-cap stocks to a small-cap value index.

PORTFOLIO 3

S&P 500 INDEX	15%
FAMA/FRENCH US LARGE VALUE INDEX (EX UTILITIES)	15%
FAMA/FRENCH US SMALL CAP INDEX	15%
FAMA/FRENCH US SMALL VALUE INDEX (EX UTILITIES)	15%
FIVE-YEAR TREASURY NOTES	40%

1975–2013

	ANNUALIZED RETURN (%)	ANNUAL STANDARD DEVIATION (%)
PORTFOLIO 1	10.8	10.6
PORTFOLIO 2	12.0	11.2
PORTFOLIO 3	12.5	12.3

STEP 3: Our next step is to shift half of our stock allocation to international stocks. For exposure to international value and international small-cap stocks we will add a 15 percent allocation to both the MSCI EAFE Value Index and the Dimensional International Small Cap Index.

PORTFOLIO 4

S&P 500 INDEX	**7.5%**
FAMA/FRENCH US LARGE VALUE INDEX (EX UTILITIES)	**7.5%**
FAMA/FRENCH US SMALL CAP INDEX	**7.5%**
FAMA/FRENCH US SMALL VALUE INDEX (EX UTILITIES)	**7.5%**
MSCI EAFE VALUE INDEX	**15%**
DIMENSIONAL INTERNATIONAL SMALL CAP INDEX	**15%**
FIVE-YEAR TREASURY NOTES	**40%**

1975–2013

	ANNUALIZED RETURN (%)	ANNUAL STANDARD DEVIATION (%)
PORTFOLIO 1	10.8	10.6
PORTFOLIO 2	12.0	11.2
PORTFOLIO 3	12.5	12.3
PORTFOLIO 4	12.5	11.5

The effect of the changes has been to increase the return on the portfolio from 10.8 percent to 12.5 percent. This outcome is what we should have expected to see as we added riskier small-cap and value stocks to our portfolio. Thus, we also need to consider how the risk of the portfolio was impacted by the changes. The standard deviation (a measure of volatility, or risk) of the portfolio increased from 10.6 percent to 11.5 percent.

You have now seen the power of modern portfolio theory at work. You saw how you can add risky (and, therefore, higher expected returning) assets to a portfolio and increase the returns more than the risks were increased. That is the benefit of diversification across asset classes that are not perfectly correlated. While most investors and advisors with this knowledge have used it in the above manner, there is another way to consider using it. Instead of trying to increase returns without proportionally increasing risk, we can try to achieve the same return while lowering the risk of the portfolio. To achieve this goal we increase the bond allocation to 60 percent from 40 percent and proportionally decrease the allocations to each of the equity asset classes.

PORTFOLIO 5

S&P 500 INDEX	**5%**
FAMA/FRENCH US LARGE VALUE INDEX (EX UTILITIES)	**5%**
FAMA/FRENCH US SMALL CAP INDEX	**5%**
FAMA/FRENCH US SMALL VALUE INDEX (EX UTILITIES)	**5%**
DIMENSIONAL INTERNATIONAL SMALL CAP INDEX	**10%**
MSCI EAFE VALUE INDEX	**10%**
FIVE-YEAR TREASURY NOTES	**60%**

1975–2013

	ANNUALIZED RETURN (%)	ANNUAL STANDARD DEVIATION (%)
PORTFOLIO 1	10.8	10.6
PORTFOLIO 2	12.0	11.2
PORTFOLIO 3	12.5	12.3
PORTFOLIO 4	12.5	11.5
PORTFOLIO 5	11.0	8.1

Compared with Portfolio 1, Portfolio 5 achieved a higher return with far less risk. Portfolio 5 provided a 0.2 percent higher return, 11.0 percent versus 10.8 percent. It did so while experiencing 2.5 percent lower volatility, 8.1 percent versus 10.6 percent.

Now that you have a good understanding of how modern portfolio theory can be used to build more efficient portfolios, we will move to our last step — showing you how, by concentrating your equity allocation in only the highest expected returning asset classes, you can improve a portfolio's risk profile even further, making it look more like the original Portfolio B than the original Portfolio A. Recalling the two portfolios from earlier in the book, A and B, we will show you how to build a portfolio that looks a lot more like B (the one you preferred) than A.

Just as the equity premium is compensation for taking risk, so are the size and value premiums. Thus, we add the usual disclaimer that the future may look different from the past. There are no guarantees in investing.

Due to data limitations the period we will now consider is the 31-year period 1982–2013. We will look at two portfolios, A and B. Portfolio A has the same typical allocation of 60 percent S&P 500 Index/40 percent five-year Treasury notes. Portfolio B will hold 25 percent stocks and 75 percent five-year Treasury notes. With U.S. stocks representing roughly half of the global equity market capitalization, we will split the equity allocation equally between U.S. small value stocks (using the Fama-French Small Value Index) and international small value stocks (using the Dimensional Small Cap Value Index).

1982–2013

	PORTFOLIO A	PORTFOLIO B
ANNUALIZED RETURNS / STANDARD DEVIATION (%)	10.7/10.7	10.3/7.1
YEARS WITH RETURNS ABOVE 15% / BELOW –15%	11/1	9/0
YEARS WITH RETURNS ABOVE 20% / BELOW –20%	7/0	2/0
YEARS WITH RETURNS ABOVE 25% / BELOW–25%	2/0	2/0
WORST YEAR RETURN / BEST YEAR RETURN (%)	–17.0/29.3	–2.3/28.0
NUMBER OF YEARS WITH NEGATIVE RETURN	5	2

PORTFOLIO A: 60 PERCENT S&P 500 INDEX/40 PERCENT FIVE-YEAR TREASURY NOTES

PORTFOLIO B: 12.5 PERCENT FAMA-FRENCH U.S. SMALL VALUE INDEX/12.5 PERCENT DIMENSIONAL INTERNATIONAL SMALL CAP VALUE INDEX/75 PERCENT FIVE-YEAR TREASURY NOTES

As you can see, Portfolio B produced similar returns to Portfolio A. However, it did so while experiencing volatility that was 3.6 percentage points less — 7.1 percent versus 10.7 percent. In addition, it had fewer returns in the tails (both the extreme good and bad returns). While Portfolio A had 11 years with returns greater than 15 percent, Portfolio B had nine. And while Portfolio A had one year with a loss greater than 15 percent, Portfolio B never experienced a loss that large. Moving the hurdle to the 20 percent level, we see that while Portfolio A had seven years with returns greater than that level and no years with losses of that size, Portfolio B had just two years of gains that large. Moving the hurdle to the 25 percent level, both Portfolios A and B had two years with returns in excess of 25 percent and no years with losses that great. The best single year for Portfolio A was 1995 when it returned 29.3 percent. The best single year for Portfolio B was 1985 when it returned 28.0 percent. Note that while Portfolio B has just 25 percent in equities, its best year was almost as good as the best year for Portfolio A, which has 60 percent in equities. On the other hand, Portfolio A's worst single year was 2008 when it lost 17.0 percent. The worst single year for Portfolio B was 1994 when it lost just 2.3 percent. In addition, while Portfolio A experienced five years of negative returns, Portfolio B experienced just two.

As you can see, Portfolio B — the low-beta/high-tilt portfolio — with its shorter tails looks more like our original Portfolio B (the one you preferred). While its best year was not as good as Portfolio A's best year, and it had fewer years in the good right tail, its worst year was much less painful than Portfolio A's worst year, and it had fewer years in the bad right tail.

There is another important point to cover. Below is the original illustration of the potential dispersion of returns for Portfolios A and B.

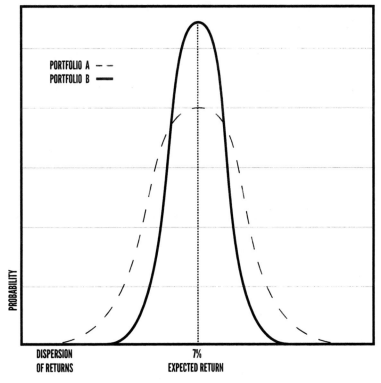

Recall your preference for Portfolio B was based on your risk aversion — your willingness to give up the opportunity for the extreme good returns in the distribution of returns in the right tail of Portfolio A in return for minimizing the risks of the extreme bad returns in its left tail. The illustration shows that both the good and bad tails of Portfolio A were reduced equally if you chose Portfolio B. However, using actual returns we saw that while Portfolio A did produce more good years than Portfolio B, and it had a higher best returning year than did Portfolio B, the difference in returns between their best years was just 1 percent, while the difference in the worst years was almost 15 percent. In other words, bad tail risk was curtailed much more than good tail risk. If you preferred Portfolio B to Portfolio A, you should have a strong preference for a low-beta/high-tilt portfolio.

Before moving on, there is one more important point we need to cover. We must admit that there is no way that in 1982 we could have predicted that the allocation for Portfolio B would have produced a very similar return as the allocation for Portfolio A. We might have guessed at a similar allocation, but we cannot predict the future with anything close to that kind of accuracy.

We have one final example to take you through. On December 23, 2011,

Ron Lieber, financial columnist for the *New York Times*, wrote an article titled "Taking a Chance on the Larry Portfolio" — and the "Larry Portfolio" (LP) was born. The LP is the "technical" term for a portfolio that basically limits its stock holdings to the highest returning equity asset classes available to individual investors in low-cost, passively managed investment vehicles — U.S. small value stocks, developed markets small value stocks and emerging markets value stocks. Limiting the stock holdings to the highest expected returning asset classes allows an investor to have a lower overall allocation to stocks and achieve the same expected return.

Due to data limitations, we now will consider the 24-year period 1989–2013. We will again look at two portfolios, A and B. Portfolio A has the same typical allocation of 60 percent S&P 500 Index/40 percent five-year Treasury notes. Portfolio B will hold 28 percent stocks and 72 percent five-year Treasury notes. (Note the change from the previous example which used 75 percent stocks and recall our disclaimer that we cannot predict with perfect accuracy what allocation will produce the same returns.) Again we split our equity holdings, with a 14 percent allocation to both domestic and international stocks. And with emerging markets stocks making up about 25 percent of the capitalization of international stocks, our international allocation becomes 10.5 percent international small value stocks and 3.5

43

percent emerging markets value stocks (using the Fama-French Emerging

Markets Value Index).

1989–2013

	PORTFOLIO A	PORTFOLIO B
ANNUALIZED RETURNS / STANDARD DEVIATION (%)	9.3/11.0	9.0/6.6
YEARS WITH RETURNS ABOVE 15% / BELOW –15%	7/1	6/0
YEARS WITH RETURNS ABOVE 20% / BELOW –20%	5/0	2/0
YEARS WITH RETURNS ABOVE 25% / BELOW –25%	1/0	0/0
WORST YEAR RETURN / BEST YEAR RETURN (%)	-17.0/29.3	-3.0/22.0
NUMBER OF YEARS WITH NEGATIVE RETURN	5	2

As you can see, the two portfolios produced almost exactly the

same return (Portfolio A returned 9.3 percent and Portfolio B returned

9.0 percent). However, Portfolio B experienced less volatility —

6.6 percent versus 11.0 percent. In addition, it generally had fewer returns

in the tails (the extreme good and bad returns). Both portfolios had six

years with returns greater than 15 percent. However, while Portfolio A

had one year with a loss of greater than 15 percent, Portfolio B never

experienced a loss that large. Moving the hurdle to the 20 percent level,

we see that while Portfolio A had five years with returns greater than

that level and no years with losses of that size, Portfolio B had just two years of returns above 20 percent. Moving the hurdle to the 25 percent level, Portfolio A had one year with a return in excess of 25 percent and no years with losses that great. Portfolio B did not experience a year with a loss or gain of that amount or greater. The best single year for Portfolio A was 1995 when it returned 29.3 percent. The best single year for Portfolio B was 2003 when it returned 22.0 percent. Note that while Portfolio B has just 28 percent in equities, its best year's return was only 7.3 percent lower than Portfolio A's best year. On the other hand, in 2008, the worst year for both portfolios, Portfolio B lost just 3 percent, 14 percentage points less than Portfolio A's loss of 17.0 percent. In addition, while Portfolio A experienced five years of negative returns, Portfolio B experienced just two. If you are like most investors you would have been sleeping much better with Portfolio B than with Portfolio A.

Experience has taught us that limiting the risk of large losses increases the odds that you will be able to maintain discipline during bear markets, thereby avoiding the panicked selling that destroys the odds of achieving your financial goals.

The next section addresses a question we are often asked: Is the "Larry Portfolio" well diversified?

CHAPTER 4:
IS THE "LARRY PORTFOLIO"
WELL DIVERSIFIED?

While the LP has earned superior risk-adjusted returns (producing a higher Sharpe ratio than that of a market-like portfolio, with much smaller worst-case losses), one concern investors have expressed is that "it is not well diversified." In one sense that is a true statement. The LP does limit the stock holdings in both the U.S. and developed international markets to small value stocks, and in emerging markets to value stocks. That means there are no U.S. and international developed markets holdings of small-cap, mid-cap and large-cap growth companies, and no holding of mid-cap and large-cap value companies. And in emerging markets there are no growth stocks, just value stocks.

To answer the question of whether the LP is well diversified, we need to have you think about diversification in a different way than you are probably used to. The conventional way of thinking about how well a portfolio is diversified is to think in terms of the number and weighting of individual stocks, asset classes and geographic regions. We want you to also think about diversification in terms exposure to the factors that determine the risk and return of a portfolio.

As we have discussed, to understand how markets work financial economists have developed what are called factor models. The standard model used is the Fama-French three-factor model. Again, the three factors are beta (exposure to the risk of the stock market), size (exposure to the risk of small-cap stocks) and value (exposure to the risk of value stocks). To answer the question about how well a highly tilted portfolio is diversified, we will begin by looking at the exposure a total stock market fund (portfolio) has to the three factors.

A total stock market (TSM) fund has by definition an exposure to beta of 1. However, while a TSM fund holds small-cap stocks it has no exposure at all to the size factor. This seeming contradiction confuses many investors. The reason for the confusion is that factors are long/short portfolios. The size factor is the return of small-cap stocks *minus* the return of large-cap stocks. In other words, small-cap stocks provide a *positive* exposure to the size effect and large-cap stocks provide a *negative* exposure to it. Thus, while the small-cap stocks in TSM funds provide *positive* exposure to the size factor, the large-cap stocks in TSM funds provide an exactly offsetting amount of *negative* exposure. That puts the *net* exposure to the size factor at 0. The same is true for value stocks. The value factor is the return of value stocks *minus* the return of growth stocks. Value stocks provide a *positive* exposure to the value effect and growth stocks a *negative* exposure. While the value stocks within TSM funds provide *positive* exposure to the value factor, the growth stocks in TSM funds provide an exactly offsetting amount of *negative* exposure. That puts the *net* exposure to the value factor at 0.

We now turn to looking at the exposures that the LP has to the factors. While the exact answer depends on which funds are used to implement the strategy (the smaller the weighted average market capitalization of the stocks in the fund, and the lower their weighted average price-to-book ratio, the greater the exposure to the factors), the funds in the portfolios we use to build the LP create a portfolio with loadings (exposure to the factors) on the size and value factors of approximately 0.6. And like most well-diversified stock portfolios the equity portion of the portfolio has a beta of about 1.

Now consider a portfolio that uses the high-tilt, low-beta approach of the LP and has a 30 percent allocation to stocks. The portfolio will have a beta of about 0.3, a size loading of about 0.18 (0.6 x 0.3) and a value loading of about 0.18 (0.6 x 0.3). And the portfolio's bond holdings will give it exposure to term risk as well — how much will depend on the maturity of the bonds used for the bond portion of the portfolio. Thus, the portfolio has exposure to four factors, each of which has low correlation to the other factors. Contrast that with a TSM portfolio with a 100 percent allocation to stocks. It has a beta of 1, and that is the only factor to which it is exposed.

Thus, while a TSM fund is more diversified when you think about diversification across asset classes (holding more equity asset classes/ filling in more of Morningstar's style boxes), the LP is more diversified when looking at exposures to risk factors. A TSM fund has all of its eggs in one risk basket — beta — while the LP diversifies its risks across three stock risk baskets — beta, size and value, and the term factor of the bond holdings as well. The LP is also just as diversified in terms of economic and geopolitical risks across countries. And it certainly holds a sufficient number of stocks. Using the international small value and emerging markets value funds of DFA and Bridgeway's Omni Small Value

Fund, it holds the stocks of about 4,800 companies from 43 countries — certainly more than enough to diversify away any idiosyncratic risks. In fact, it holds just about the same number of stocks as Vanguard's Total World Stock Index Fund which holds about 4,900 from 41 countries.

The bottom line is that the LP is a well-diversified portfolio, just not so well-diversified when thought of in a traditional *asset class* approach. And while that leaves the investor subject to that dreaded psychological disease known as tracking error regret — the portfolio's returns will look very different from those of the market — the benefits in terms of reduced tail risk are large in comparison.

CHAPTER 5:
CONCLUSION

We hope that you have found the journey you have taken with us both informative and of great value. After all, the Holy Grail of investing is the search for investment strategies that can deliver higher expected returns without increased risk or the same expected return with reduced risk — and we have shown you the road map to it. The road map comes with the following "directions."

- Current stock valuations play an important role in determining future returns. Thus, they should be used (not historical returns) to help determine the expected return of a portfolio. The Shiller CAPE 10 is a useful metric to help estimate future returns.

- The expected return should be considered only the mean

of a wide dispersion of potential returns. Your plan should incorporate options (such as staying in the work force longer, moving to a location with a lower cost of living and so on) that you will adopt in order to minimize the risk of failure, regardless of which potential outcome becomes reality.

- Think about diversification in terms of the factors (instead of asset classes) that explain returns, diversifying the risks across those factors.

- To the extent you are willing to accept the risk of tracking error regret, concentrate the equity portion of your portfolio in the highest expected returning asset classes. All else equal (for example, expense ratios), use funds that have the highest loadings (exposure) to the factors. That allows you to minimize your exposure to beta which is the biggest risk factor.

- Diversify the portfolio across the globe. For example, the equity portion of the portfolio might have a 50 percent allocation to U.S. small value stocks, a 37.5 percent allocation to international developed markets small value stocks and a 12.5 percent allocation to emerging markets value stocks.

We also offer an important caution. Just as we can only estimate the future return of the stock market, we can only estimate what future return to small value stocks will be. History and current valuations provide a guide, helping us to make estimates. However, all crystal balls are cloudy — there are no guarantees. What we do know is that a low-beta/high-tilt portfolio does reduce the risk of the fat tails (both good and bad). However, we cannot guarantee that it will produce the same return as a more market-like portfolio with a higher equity allocation.

Your journey with us is not quite over. The appendices that follow address the following three important topics:

- The use of Monte Carlo simulation in determining your asset allocation.

- Since Fama and French's work on their three factor model, academics have "discovered" three other factors that not only help explain the differences in returns of diversified portfolios, but also carry premiums. The three additional factors are momentum, profitability and investment.

- Not all index and passively managed funds are created equal. Even two passively managed funds within the same asset class (such as U.S. small value) can have very different portfolio construction rules which lead to different loadings (exposure to the factors) and different expected returns.

- The importance of knowing when you have enough.

APPENDIX A:
MONTE CARLO [MC] SIMULATION

MC simulations require a set of assumptions regarding time horizon, initial investment, asset allocation, withdrawals, savings, retirement income, rate of inflation, correlation among the different asset classes and — very importantly — the return distributions of the portfolio.

In MC simulation programs, the growth of an investment portfolio is determined by two important inputs: portfolio average expected return and portfolio volatility, represented by the standard deviation measure. Based on these two inputs, the MC simulation program generates a sequence of random returns from which one return is applied in each year of the simulation. This process is repeated thousands of times to calculate the likelihood of possible outcomes and their potential distributions.

MC simulations also provide another important benefit: They allow investors to view the outcomes of various strategies and how marginal changes in asset allocations change the odds of these outcomes. We'll examine the results of a hypothetical investor. An initial withdrawal is made equal to the specified withdrawal rate times $1 million. The remaining assets then grow or shrink per the asset returns in the replication for that year. At the end of the year, the portfolio is rebalanced back to the target allocation. In subsequent years, the withdrawal is the prior year's withdrawals plus inflation for that year. Withdrawals are made at the start of each year. It is assumed that taxes are included in the withdrawal amount.

This section will look at portfolios with various hypothetical equity versus fixed income allocations, as well as various tilts to small-cap and value stocks. Three measures will be examined:

1. The success rate, which is the probability that the portfolio has at least one dollar at the end of the planning horizon. Of course, if someone has a 95 percent success rate, this also means they have a 5 percent chance of failure.

2. The portfolio value at the fifth percentile based on a $1 million initial portfolio value. This will be reported in today's dollars at the end of the retirement period. If the portfolio depletes at the fifth percentile, we examine when the portfolio depletes.

3. The portfolio value at the 50th percentile based on a $1 million initial portfolio value. This will be reported in today's dollars at the end of the retirement period. In half of the cases, investors should expect greater than this value, and in half of the cases the investor should expect less.

These outcomes are calculated from 10,000 MC simulations over a 30-year horizon. We will review the results using three different withdrawal rates: 3 percent, 4 percent and 5 percent. We will examine three hypothetical asset allocations:

*   **PORTFOLIO A:**
    60 percent total stock market/40 percent fixed income

*   **PORTFOLIO B:**
    60 percent equity tilted to small-cap and value/40 percent fixed income

*   **PORTFOLIO C:**
    40 percent equity tilted to small-cap and value/60 percent fixed income.

The portfolios tilted to small-cap and value load 0.5 on size and 0.2 on value.

The table below shows the real return capital market expectations used in the 10,000 MC simulations. It is important to note that the results from any MC simulation will be based on the inputs used. If we were to use different capital markets assumptions, the results in the tables that follow would be very different.

CAPITAL MARKETS ASSUMPTIONS

	ARITHMETIC MEAN REAL RETURN (%)	STANDARD DEVIATION (%)
TOTAL STOCK MARKET EQUITY	4.8	18.1
TILTED EQUITY PORTFOLIO	6.5	20.7
FIXED INCOME	1.1	4.1
INFLATION	2.2	

RESULTS: 3 PERCENT WITHDRAWAL RATE

ASSET ALLOCATION	SUCCESS RATE (%)
PORTFOLIO A	94
PORTFOLIO B	95
PORTFOLIO C	98

EQUITY ALLOCATION	5TH PERCENTILE RESULTS
PORTFOLIO A	DEPLETES YEAR 29
PORTFOLIO B	$9,915
PORTFOLIO C	$118,699

EQUITY ALLOCATION	50TH PERCENTILE RESULTS
PORTFOLIO A	$794,086
PORTFOLIO B	$1,176,922
PORTFOLIO C	$872,111

At a relatively low 3 percent withdrawal rate, changes in asset allocation do not have a significant effect on success rates. However, someone who is highly risk averse and worried about the bottom fifth percentile of cases may wish to tilt more to size and value and reduce the portfolio's equity allocation. On the other hand, someone who has a goal of leaving a larger estate may want to keep the portfolio's 60/40 asset allocation but tilt the equity portion to small-cap and value stocks (as evidenced by the 50th percentile results).

RESULTS: 4 PERCENT WITHDRAWAL RATE

ASSET ALLOCATION	SUCCESS RATE (%)
PORTFOLIO A	72
PORTFOLIO B	79
PORTFOLIO C	80

EQUITY ALLOCATION	5TH PERCENTILE RESULTS
PORTFOLIO A	DEPLETES YEAR 23
PORTFOLIO B	DEPLETES YEAR 23
PORTFOLIO C	DEPLETES YEAR 25

EQUITY ALLOCATION	50TH PERCENTILE RESULTS
PORTFOLIO A	$325,969
PORTFOLIO B	$626,895
PORTFOLIO C	$391,511

At a 4 percent withdrawal rate, we see significant improvement in success rates by tilting the equity portfolio to small-cap and value stocks.

Further, at the fifth percentile, the portfolio that tilts toward small and value while reducing the equity allocation runs out of money later in the analysis. Again, investors who wish to leave a large estate should maintain their equity allocation but tilt the portfolio to small-cap and value stocks.

RESULTS: 5 PERCENT WITHDRAWAL RATE

ASSET ALLOCATION	SUCCESS RATE (%)
PORTFOLIO A	42
PORTFOLIO B	55
PORTFOLIO C	44

EQUITY ALLOCATION	5TH PERCENTILE RESULTS
PORTFOLIO A	DEPLETES YEAR 17
PORTFOLIO B	DEPLETES YEAR 18
PORTFOLIO C	DEPLETES YEAR 19

EQUITY ALLOCATION	50TH PERCENTILE RESULTS
PORTFOLIO A	DEPLETES YEAR 29
PORTFOLIO B	$97,328
PORTFOLIO C	DEPLETES YEAR 29

At a relatively high withdrawal rate (5 percent), no amount of changes in the asset allocation will get the investor to an acceptable success rate. This investor should either reduce spending, plan on working longer, lower the goal or find other sources of income.

APPENDIX B:
OTHER KNOWN SOURCES OF RETURN

MOMENTUM

A momentum-based strategy buys stocks that have done relatively well over the past 12 months and shorts stocks that have had relatively poor returns over the same period. Jegadeesh and Titman are credited in academia for discovering momentum in their paper "Returns to Buying Winners and Selling Losers" in *The Journal of Finance* in 1993. This paper found that recent (3–12 months) relative winners will continue to be relative winners over the next 3–12 months and recent relative losers will continue to be relative losers over the next 3–12 months. They found that after 12 months, the effect disappears.

In 1994, Cliff Asness, as part of his PhD dissertation titled "Variables that Explain Stock Returns," found that long-term winners eventually become growth stocks that underperform and long-term losers eventually become value stocks that subsequently outperform. This was one of the first papers that argued that value and momentum are related.

In 1996, Eugene Fama and Kenneth French compared all of the market anomalies known at the time to the Fama-French three-factor model. They found that the only anomaly to survive and not be captured by the size and value effects was momentum.

In 1997, Cliff Asness explored the relationship between value and momentum strategies further in a paper published in the *Financial Analysts Journal*. He found that value tends to be strongest among low-momentum stocks and weakest among high-momentum stocks. He also found that momentum strategies work across the value-versus-growth spectrum.

Also in 1997, Mark Carhart augmented the Fama-French three-factor model with a fourth factor based on momentum. This new momentum factor made a large contribution to the explanatory power of the model. He also found that momentum stocks are correlated with each other.

The most commonly cited concern regarding following a momentum strategy centers around transaction costs. A momentum strategy creates high turnover. This raises the question of whether the momentum premium survives in the "real world" with real trading costs. The 2012 paper by Andrea Frazzini, Ronen Israel and Tobias J. Moskowitz, "Trading Costs of Asset Pricing Anomalies," found that the actual trading costs are low enough to allow for the momentum premium to survive.

PROFITABILITY

A June 2012 study by Robert Novy-Marx, "The Other Side of Value: The Gross Profitability Premium," provided investors with new insights into the cross-section of stock returns. The study used Compustat data covering the period 1962–2010, and employed accounting data for a given fiscal year starting at the end of June of the following calendar year. The findings may shake up the way value investors construct portfolios. The following is a summary of the author's findings:

- Profitable firms generate significantly higher returns than unprofitable firms, despite having significantly higher valuation ratios (higher price-to-book ratios).

- Profitable firms tend to be growth firms — they grow faster. Gross profitability is a powerful predictor of future growth in gross profitability, earnings, free cash flow and payouts.

- The most profitable firms earn 0.31 percent per month higher average returns than the least profitable firms. The data is statistically significant (t-statistic of 2.49).

- Controlling for profitability dramatically increases the performance of value strategies, especially among the largest, most liquid stocks. And controlling for book-to-market improves the performance of profitability strategies.

- Because both gross-profits-to-assets and book-to-market are highly persistent, turnover of the strategies is relatively low.

- Because strategies based on profitability are growth strategies, they provide an excellent hedge for value strategies — adding profitability on top of a value strategy reduces the strategy's overall volatility because the two strategies are negatively correlated.

As further evidence that the two strategies combine well, consider the following: While both the profitability and value strategies generally performed well over the sample, both had significant periods in which they lost money. Profitability performed poorly from the mid-1970s to the early 1980s and over the middle of the 2000s, while value performed poorly over the 1990s. However, profitability generally performed well in the periods when value performed poorly and vice versa. As a result, the mixed profitability-value strategy never experienced a losing five-year period.

The author also tested the strategies in international markets and found similar results, providing an out-of-sample test. The period covered was July 1990 through October 2009 and included 19 developed market countries.

INVESTMENT

The authors of the September 2012 study "Digesting Anomalies: An Investment Approach," which covers the period 1972–2011, proposed a new multifactor model that goes a long way to explaining many of the anomalies that neither the Fama-French three-factor model nor the Carhart four-factor model (adding momentum as the fourth factor) can explain. In the new model (which they call the q-factor model), the expected return of an asset in excess of the riskless rate is described by the sensitivity of its return to four factors — three of which we have already discussed (beta, size and profitability). Their innovation was to introduce an investment factor — the difference between the return on a portfolio of low-investment stocks and the return on a portfolio of high-investment stocks. They found that the investment factor earns an average return of 0.44 percent per month and is statistically significant. They also found that the investment factor is highly correlated with the value premium (0.69), suggesting that this factor plays a similar role to that of the value factor.

APPENDIX C:
HOW TO EVALUATE INDEX
AND PASSIVE FUNDS

For evidence-based investors the choice is much simpler than it is for active investors because the universe of funds from which to choose is much smaller. However, even for evidence-based investors the choice is not as simple as just looking at the expense ratios of the various alternatives within each asset class and choosing the cheapest alternative. The reason is that not all "index" funds are created equal.

While the expense ratio is an important consideration, it should not be the only one. The reason is that a fund manager can add value in several ways that have nothing to do with "active" investing (active investing being defined as the use of either technical or fundamental analysis to identify specific securities to either over- or underweight).

Let's explore some of the ways a fund can add value in terms of portfolio construction, tax management and/or trading strategies.

1. CHOICE OF BENCHMARK INDEX OR HOW A FUND DEFINES ITS INVESTMENT UNIVERSE

This decision impacts returns in several important ways.

- Turnover, which impacts trading costs and tax efficiency. Some indices have higher turnover than others. And some indices/funds have added hold ranges (the index/ fund will no longer buy additional shares, but it will not sell existing holdings) that are designed to reduce the negative impact of turnover (both on transaction costs and tax efficiency).

- Exposure to the risk factors of size and value — the greater the exposure, the higher the risk and expected return of the fund.

As an example, let us look at two such funds: the DFA US Small Cap Value Portfolio (DFSVX) and the Vanguard Small-Cap Value Index Fund (VSIAX). The table shows their expense ratios and degrees of exposure to the market, size and value premiums for the period January 2009–December 2013.

	MARKET PREMIUM EXPOSURE	SIZE PREMIUM EXPOSURE	VALUE PREMIUM EXPOSURE	EXPENSE RATIO
DFSVX	1.09	0.92	0.39	0.52%
VSIAX	1.01	0.64	0.41	0.10%

The point is not to say that one fund is necessarily better than the other. The lesson here is that not all passive funds are created equal, and you should not simply look at the expense ratio and end the evaluation. Instead, determine how much exposure you need to the market, size and value premiums and find the least expensive way of getting that exposure. And remember that the more exposure you have to the size and value premiums, the less equity risk you need to hold to achieve the same expected return.

- Correlation of the fund to the other portfolio assets (the lower the correlation, the more effective the diversification).

- Some indices are more opaque than others, preventing actively managed funds from exploiting the "forced turnover" that is created when indices are reconstituted (typically annually). The lack of opaqueness has historically created problems for index funds that replicate the Russell 2000 Index.

- A fund can add value by incorporating the momentum effect by temporarily delaying the purchase of stocks that are exhibiting negative momentum and by temporarily delaying the sale of stocks exhibiting positive momentum. It can also add value by incorporating the profitability factor.

- A fund can screen out certain securities (even if they are within the defined index) that have characteristics that have demonstrated poor risk/return characteristics (such as stocks in bankruptcy, very low-priced stocks, IPOs or extreme small growth stocks). For example, while utilities and real estate stocks typically have high book-to-market ratios (and, therefore, are found in most value indices), they have very low betas (exposure to equity risk). The result is that their inclusion in value indices that use book-to-market as the screen creates a drag on returns. In addition, the inclusion of real estate in value funds will make the fund less tax efficient (since the dividends from REITs are non-qualified and thus taxed as ordinary income).

- How often an index reconstitutes can impact returns. Most indices (such as the Russell and RAFI Fundamental Indices) reconstitute annually. The lack of frequent reconstitution can create significant style drift. For example, from 1990 through 2006 the percentage of stocks in the Russell 2000 in June that would leave the index when it reconstituted at the end of the month was 20 percent. For the Russell 2000 Value Index the figure was 28 percent. The result is that over the course of the year a small-cap index fund based on the Russell 2000 would have seen its exposure to the size factor drift lower over the course of the year. For small value funds based on the Russell 2000 Value Index, their exposure to both the small and value premiums would have drifted lower. The drift toward lower exposure to the risk factors results in lower expected returns.

2. PATIENT TRADING

If a fund's goal is to replicate an index, it must trade when stocks enter or exit an index and it must also hold the exact weighting of each security in the index. A fund with a goal to earn the return of the asset class and that is willing to live with some random tracking error relative to its benchmark index can be more patient in its trading strategy, using market orders and block trading that can take advantage of discounts offered by active managers that desire to quickly sell large blocks of stock. Patient trading reduces transaction costs and block trading can even create negative trading costs in some cases.

3. TAX MANAGEMENT

While indexing is a relatively tax efficient strategy (due to relatively low turnover), there are ways to improve the tax efficiency of a fund.

- Harvest losses whenever they are significant.

- Eliminate any unintentional short-term capital gains (those that are not the result of acquisitions).

- Create wider buy and hold ranges in order to reduce turnover.

- Preserve qualified dividends. A fund must own the stock that earns the dividends for more than 60 days of a prescribed 121-day period. That period begins 60 days prior to the ex-dividend date.

- Limit securities lending revenue to the expense ratio.

4. MULTIPLE VALUE SCREENS

It is well documented in the academic research on stock returns that value stocks have outperformed growth stocks. And we see the higher returns to value stocks in almost all countries (with Japan being a notable exception). Not only has value outperformed growth, but the persistence of its outperformance has been greater than the persistence of stocks outperforming bonds.

When implementing a value strategy, many different metrics can be used. Among the most common are price-to-earnings, price-to-sales, price-to-book-value, price-to-dividends and price-to-cash-flow. All the various metrics produce results showing that value stocks have had higher returns than growth stocks. And the various measures produce similar results (with the weakest results coming from the use of the price-to-dividend ratio).

Given the similarity in results, the price-to-book ratio has been used the most because book value is more stable over time than the other metrics. That helps keep portfolio turnover down, which in turn keeps trading costs down and tax efficiency higher. Recently, some passively managed funds have moved away from the single-screen metric as their research indicates that using multiple screens produces better results. The reasoning here is that price-to-book can work well as a value metric in some industries/sectors but not others. With this in mind, it could make sense to use multiple value metrics instead of sorting exclusively by price-to-book.

5. SECURITIES LENDING

Securities lending refers to the lending of securities by one party to another. Securities are often borrowed with the intent to sell them short. In the international markets there is another reason for securities lending to occur that has to do with the ability to utilize the foreign tax credit. Thus, the opportunities to add value are greater in foreign markets. As payment for the loan of the security, the parties negotiate a fee. Some mutual funds are more aggressive than others in this area.

The following example demonstrates why it is a mistake to only look at the fund's operating expense ratio. Let us assume that Fund A has an expense ratio of 55 basis points and it generates 40 basis points in securities lending fees. Thus, we might consider the fund's net expenses to be 15 basis points. Fund B in the same asset class has an expense ratio that is significantly lower at 35 basis points. However, it generated just 12 basis points in lending fees. Thus, its net expenses of 23 basis points exceeded the 15 basis points net expense of Fund A. Securities lending revenue data is available in the annual reports of mutual funds.

6. CORE FUNDS

Core funds combine multiple asset classes into a single fund. A core approach was developed because it is the most efficient way to hold multiple asset classes, especially for taxable accounts. The following example will demonstrate why this is the case.

The Russell 3000 can be broken down into four components. The 500 stocks that make up the Russell 1000 Growth Index, the 500 stocks that make up the Russell 1000 Value Index, the 1,000 stocks that make up the Russell 2000 Growth Index and the 1,000 stocks in the Russell 2000 Value Index. We have seen institutions that have held all four components in exactly the same market cap weighting that the Russell 3000 holds them. In other words, they owned the same stocks, in the very same proportions, as did the Russell 3000 — only in four funds instead of one. This makes no sense because when the indices reconstitute each June, each of the four component index funds will have to sell the stocks that leave its index and buy the stocks that enter its index. That incurs transaction costs, which can be particularly large when the entire market knows you have to trade, and especially large for small-cap stocks. The benefits of owning the single fund are obvious.

Another example of a core fund is the Vanguard Total International Stock Index Fund which combines holdings in developed and emerging markets. This is a significant improvement for investors who previously would have had to hold the two components separately. A single fund will avoid having to sell and buy the stocks from a country that migrates from emerging to developed markets as Israel recently did, and as South Korea and Taiwan are expected to do. This not only minimizes transaction costs in markets where they can be quite high, but it also avoids, or at least minimizes, the realization of capital gains. It also eliminates the need for the investor to rebalance the portfolio, avoiding trading costs and the realization of capital gains. The fund itself rebalances with "other people's money," using cash flows and dividends to rebalance.

Now consider an investor who owns four component U.S. index funds, a large company fund, a small company fund, a large value fund and a small value fund. If there existed a single fund that held the same stocks, in the same proportions, that would be a more efficient approach. DFA has created core funds with various degrees of tilts (more than market-cap weightings) to small-cap and value stocks. Again, the benefits are reduced turnover — which reduces transaction costs and the realization of capital gains — and the minimization of the need to rebalance. Each of these can provide significant benefits, especially for taxable accounts.

Core portfolios are just another example of how financial engineering can add value by structure, without trying to add value (with low odds of success) by generating alpha from stock picking or market timing strategies.

SUMMARY

The way to see things right is in the whole. While certain funds can be the cheapest in terms of expense ratios, when evaluating similar passively managed mutual funds it is important to consider not only the operating expense ratio, but also all the ways that a fund can add value. A little bit of extra homework can pay significant dividends.

APPENDIX D: ENOUGH

To know you have enough is to be rich.

—The Tao Te Ching

Author Kurt Vonnegut related this story about fellow author Joseph Heller: "Heller and I were at a party given by a billionaire on Shelter Island. I said, 'Joe, how does it make you feel to know that our host only yesterday may have made more money than your novel *Catch-22* has earned in its entire history?' Joe said, 'I've got something he can never have.' And I said, 'What on earth could that be, Joe?' And Joe said, 'The knowledge that I've got *enough.*'"

What Heller was saying was that you are rich when you know that you have enough. Of course, everyone's definition of enough is different. From the perspective of an investment plan, how you define enough is of great importance as it defines your need to take risk — the rate of return you need to achieve your financial goal. The more you convert *desires* (what might be called "nice to haves") into *needs* ("must haves"), the larger the portfolio you will need to support that lifestyle. And the more risk you will need to take to achieve that goal.

Those with sufficient wealth to meet all their needs should consider that the strategy to get rich is entirely different from the strategy to stay rich. The strategy to get rich is to take risks, and concentrate them, typically in one's own business. However, the strategy to stay rich is to minimize risk, diversify the risks you take and to avoid spending too much. In other words, if you have already won the game — have a large enough portfolio to meet all your needs — it's time to change strategy and develop a new investment plan. The new plan should be based on the fact that the inconvenience of going from having enough to not having enough is unthinkable.

When deciding on the appropriate asset allocation, investors should consider their *marginal utility of wealth* — how much any potential incremental wealth is worth relative to the risk that must be accepted in order to achieve a greater *expected* return. While more money is always better than less, at some point most people achieve a lifestyle with which they are very comfortable. At that point, taking on incremental risk to achieve a higher net worth no longer makes sense: The potential damage of an unexpected negative outcome far exceeds the potential benefit gained from incremental wealth. The utility curve below illustrates this point.

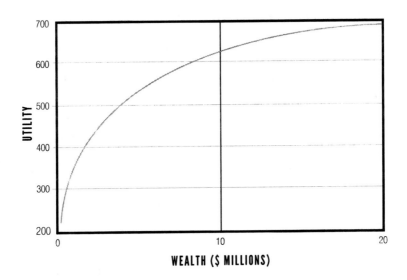

Each investor needs to decide at what level of wealth their unique utility of wealth curve starts flattening out and begins bending sharply to the right. In the above example, that point is about $10 million. For you it might be $500,000 or $1 million. There is no one right answer. Just an answer that is right for each individual. However, whether the figure is $1 million or $50 million, beyond this point there is little reason to take incremental risk to achieve a higher *expected* return. Many wealthy investors have experienced devastating losses (does the name Madoff ring a bell?) that could easily have been avoided if they had the wisdom to know what author Joseph Heller knew.

The lesson about knowing when enough is enough can be learned from the following incident. In early 2003, Larry met with a 71-year-old couple with financial assets of $3 million. Three years earlier their portfolio was worth $13 million. The only way they could have experienced that kind of loss was if they had held a portfolio that was almost all equities and heavily concentrated in U.S. large-cap growth stocks, especially technology stocks. They confirmed this. They then told him they had been working with a financial advisor during this period — demonstrating that while good advice does not have to be expensive, bad advice almost always costs you dearly.

Larry asked the couple if instead of their portfolio falling almost 80 percent, it had doubled to $26 million, would that have led to any meaningful change in the quality of their lives. The response was a definitive no. Larry then noted that the experience of watching $13 million shrink to $3 million must have been very painful and that they probably had spent many sleepless nights. They agreed. He then asked why they had taken the risks they did, knowing the potential benefit was not going to change their lives very much, but a negative outcome like the one they experienced would be so painful. The wife turned to the husband and punched him, exclaiming, "I told you so!"

Some risks are not worth taking. Prudent investors don't take more risk than they have the ability, willingness or *need* to take. The important question to ask yourself is: If you've already won the game, why are you still playing?

NEEDS VS. DESIRES

One reason people continue to play a game they have already won is that they convert what were once desires (nice things to have, but not necessary to enjoy life) into needs. That increases the need to take risk. That causes an increase in the required equity allocation. And, that can lead to problems when the risks show up, as they did in 1973–74, 2000–02 and again in 2007–08.

MORAL OF THE TALE

Failing to consider the need to take risk is a mistake common to many wealthy people, especially those who became wealthy by taking large risks. However, the mistake of taking more risk than needed is not limited to the very wealthy. The question you need to ask yourself is how much money buys happiness? Most people would be surprised to find that the figure is a lot less than they think. For example, psychologists have found that once you have enough money to meet basic needs like food, shelter and health care, incremental increases have little effect on your happiness. Once you have met those requirements the good things in life (the really important things) are either free or cheap. For example, taking a walk in a park with your significant other, riding a bike, reading a book, playing bridge with friends or playing with your children/grandchildren doesn't cost very much if anything. And switching from a $20 bottle of wine to a $100 bottle of wine, or from eating in a restaurant that costs $50 for dinner for two to one that costs $500 won't really make you any happier.

When developing your investment policy statement make sure that you have differentiated between needs and desires and then carefully considered the marginal utility of incremental wealth so that you can determine if those desires are worth the incremental risks that you will have to accept. Knowing when you have enough is one of the keys to playing the winner's game in both life and investing.